DESIGNING
PARADISE

Rizzoli

NEW YORK

New York Paris London Milan

DESIGNING PARADISE

Tropical Interiors by
JUAN MONTOYA

JORGE S. ARANGO

FOREWORD BY WENDY GOODMAN

CONTENTS

FOREWORD
BY WENDY GOODMAN

I started crying midway through looking at layouts for this book, and I didn't stop until I got to the very end. What was happening? I've never cried looking at a design book. Was I having a breakdown due to the crises of our current times? Or was it that looking at so much beauty felt like a thing from the distant past— that I feared I would never again smell the sea or feel the ocean breeze? Add to that the heartbreakingly beautiful photographs of the lush interior and exterior landscapes that Juan Montoya is so famous for making. Although I had never visited any of these ravishing residential spaces, I could imagine the sensation of being in each and every extraordinary, luminous setting. The images alone conjure such a palpable sense of family and the abiding love that the best homes reflect, and that Montoya's work has always embraced.

Since the beginning of my career as a design editor, before I even met Juan, I was deeply in awe of his legend; he was one of the greatest of the greats I had hoped to meet. Now that I have had the joy of getting to know him a little bit, that awe runs even deeper, with the understanding of how his interiors are designed to become such warm and embracing environments that illustrate the potential of what a home can be. His rooms breathe the air of happiness, ready to welcome the best of times with friends and family; they invite gatherings just as much as they offer the delicious serenity of spending time alone in the refinement of their composition. Montoya's personal elegance and warmth are always reflected in his work. His genius for being able to create magical interior worlds for his clients is grounded in his deep knowledge of history and art as well as in his respect for the precious skills of artisanal talent.

Designing Paradise is a book of Montoya's houses built for pleasure, for relaxation, and for escape—a work that illustrates the dreams he has made come true for his very lucky clients. If ever we needed paradise, especially a paradise we can hold in our hands to revisit again and again, that time is now.

New Zealand glass artists Luke Jacomb and Katherine Rutecki make
cast-glass birds. Montoya installed a flock of them on the living room wall
of the apartment he created for clients in Surfside, just north of Miami.

INTRODUCTION
JUAN MONTOYA IN THE TROPICS

Juan Montoya is a living legend. He has designed all manner of modern interiors—from sprawling, luxurious Park Avenue penthouses to Parisian pieds-à-terre, Montana fishing lodges to rambling private estates (and their gardens), movie studios to resorts. His oeuvre draws on a wide vocabulary of genres so deftly cross-pollinated that they defy easy classification. Decades before it became a staple of contemporary interior design, Montoya was intertwining global art and artifacts—African, Asiatic, Central and South American—with European styles to conjure environments that telegraphed a brand of sophistication that was at once urbane *and* comfortable. At a time when we often take this kind of peripatetic salmagundi for granted, it is not a stretch to say that Montoya was one of its early and most important progenitors.

But perhaps no typology lends itself more naturally to his creative impulses than tropical residences. There is such a sense of appropriateness to place in these projects that our assumption that the designer's stylistic affinity is somehow inborn becomes inescapable. Small wonder. As a child, Montoya's family split its time between Bogotá and a rice farm in Puerto Tejada, a remote town in Colombia's department of Cauca, about a three-hour drive from Cali. While life in the city was spent around refined Louis XV and XVI furniture, he recalls, "The hacienda was very isolated. There were cows, horses, ten dogs, and it was thoroughly tropical."

Puerto Tejada was also tropical in terms of the way houses were built. "The heat and humidity gave you no choice but to consider the particulars of the locale," he says. The kitchen was separate from the

OPPOSITE AND ABOVE: Juan Montoya in his Miami Beach pied-à-terre and as a boy on the family rice farm in Puerto Tejada, Colombia.

9

house, located in its own *palapa*, a traditional shelter covered with a palm thatch roof. Rather than cluttered with furniture, spaces had to be airy in order to improve circulation. Keeping out the sun during the day's most blistering hours required curtains and shades. Screen covers were needed for the sugar bowl to keep the ants out. "All this relates eventually to how you design a space in a tropical locale," says Montoya. For instance, he explains, "Light has to be filtered through a screen of some kind, and you need to think about how you can walk into a space without dirtying everything with mud or sand. All these things come back to you to help you crystallize a great design."

Montoya's approach to tropical design was also influenced by the legacy of the Chibcha people, the indigenous population the Europeans met when they arrived in Colombia in the sixteenth century. Long assimilated into the larger Colombian culture, the Chibcha nevertheless passed down their considerable legacy of craftsmanship, particularly in the media of pottery, cotton cloth, and gold ornament. "Any time I am in a place such as Mexico, the Dominican Republic, or South American nations," says Montoya, "I feel the crafts of the area are very important in designing the spaces."

In crowded tropical metropolises—whether Montoya's own Bogotá or Miami Beach—of course, other considerations come into play. The beach and countryside lend themselves to a more rusticated, relaxed aesthetic. Folk arts, indigenous crafts, and easy-breathing linen find a natural home in these environments. Conversely, the nature of urban locales as centers of arts and culture, as well as crossroads for international commerce and banking, invites a higher degree of sophistication. Denizens of these cities want rooms that reflect their refinement and connoisseurship, and that elevate experiences of dining and socializing to something more elegant.

OPPOSITE (CLOCKWISE FROM TOP LEFT): Until recently, Montoya and his partner, Urban Karlsson, kept a one-bedroom flat in the circa 1936 Helen Mar Apartments on Miami Beach's "Millionaire's Row" between Indian Creek and the Atlantic Ocean. Montoya installed ebonized lattice panels, commonly used in tropical houses, to separate spaces without inhibiting air circulation. The chocolate-brown living room, trimmed with an Indian motif, features a grisaille painting by Ecuadorean artist Hugo Bastidas.

Montoya understands this. His urban interiors often reflect their tropical climes primarily through their color palettes: an array of blues from pale aqua to turquoise, sand tones, and lush greens. But finishes tend to be polished and reflective. Mirrors are frequently deployed to expand the confines of a high-rise apartment beyond its walls and create the reflected illusion of being surrounded by the outdoors. Fabrics can be luxurious and emanate a subtle sheen—silk, mohair, leather.

The fluidity with which he can shape-shift as needed—and with such panache—is part of what has made Montoya a celebrated name in the world of design. He is the recipient of countless accolades. He is included in the *Architectural Digest* pantheon of Deans of American Design and frequently appears on the publication's AD100 list of top designers. He has been inducted into *Interior Design*'s Hall of Fame, and he has been presented with the Legends Award from Pratt Institute and the Gold Medal of Honor from Casita Maria Center for Arts & Education (previous recipients include Audrey Hepburn, Henry Kissinger, and Oscar de la Renta). There is scarcely an important interior design magazine in which he has not appeared. His clients include the painter Fernando Botero; style maven Elsa Klensch; the American businessman Edgar Bronfman Jr.; real estate developer Paul Kanavos and his wife, Dayssi Olarte de Kanavos, as well as scores of other socialites, princes of industry, and celebrities.

This book focuses on residences owned by a handful of Montoya's storied clientele that occupy breathtaking sites in Cap Cana, Miami Beach, Punta Mita, and other idyllic oceanfront settings. As much as these homes are escapist fantasias, they are also inextricably rooted to their geographic location and their regional culture. And while their sense of luxury is palpable, so is their lack of pretension. The elegant practicality that makes the spaces functional for the families who live in them also cleverly allows the residences to be resilient to the natural conditions in which they are found.

For a Venezuelan couple, Montoya designed a house—from architecture to gardens—in Punta Cana, Dominican Republic, next door to Oscar de la Renta. It featured yellow stucco (or *perrilla*) walls, a twenty-five-foot-tall roof supported by eucalyptus columns, and British Colonial–style furniture designed by Montoya and made by Dominican craftspeople.

PORTFOLIO

CASA DE CAMPO
DOMINICAN REPUBLIC

Before the Dominican Republic's Punta Cana peninsula exploded with resorts of every variety—from accessible all-inclusives to über-exclusive private-ownership enclaves—there was the luxury resort community of Casa de Campo. Built in the 1970s on seven thousand acres of sugarcane fields and mills once owned by Gulf + Western, Casa de Campo became the "it" getaway on the island of Hispaniola. Oscar de la Renta had a house there. Presidents, movie celebrities, and magnates flocked to its golf course. Today, it is a barefoot luxury destination for music figures such as Alicia Keyes, Rihanna, and Marc Anthony; sports stars Michael Jordan and Derek Jeter; and former Presidents Bush and Clinton.

It is also a vacation retreat for the Santo Domingo–based couple who owns this compound, as well as a destination for their children and extended family, many of whom also built houses in Casa de Campo. The large brood of relatives is close-knit and enjoys nothing so much as gathering en masse for fun, food, and drink. They embody the credo of Palm Beach socialite and fashion designer Lilly Pulitzer: "That's what life is all about: Let's have a party. Let's have it tonight."

"The clients wanted a place where they could entertain; it is a focal point of their existence here," says Montoya of the owners who erected this compilation of palm-thatch palapas with sun-bleached white fascia and columns of the fossil-rich marine stone coralina. "My vision for it had to do with how the elements that cater to that lifestyle unfold," Montoya explains. Visitors enter through massive sculpted wooden doors sheathed in glossy white lacquer that were designed, along with their hefty bronze hardware, by Montoya. Inside, just beyond the center hall table, we are at water's edge—a pool tiled in thousands of gleaming cobalt blue mosaic tesserae. Across the water, seemingly floating like an island, is the outdoor living room palapa and, beyond that, the Caribbean Sea. This is the

Steps made of coralina—a versatile and varied coral-colored stone from the Caribbean containing fossils and shells—lead to the grand double front doors, which were designed by Montoya. "I wanted the doors to have a sense of distinction," he says of the sculpted and white-lacquered forms, which he flanked with a refined take on an island staple: bamboo wattle. Visitors also pass between fragrant potted olive trees in massive planters. Across the threshold one encounters distant views of the ocean.

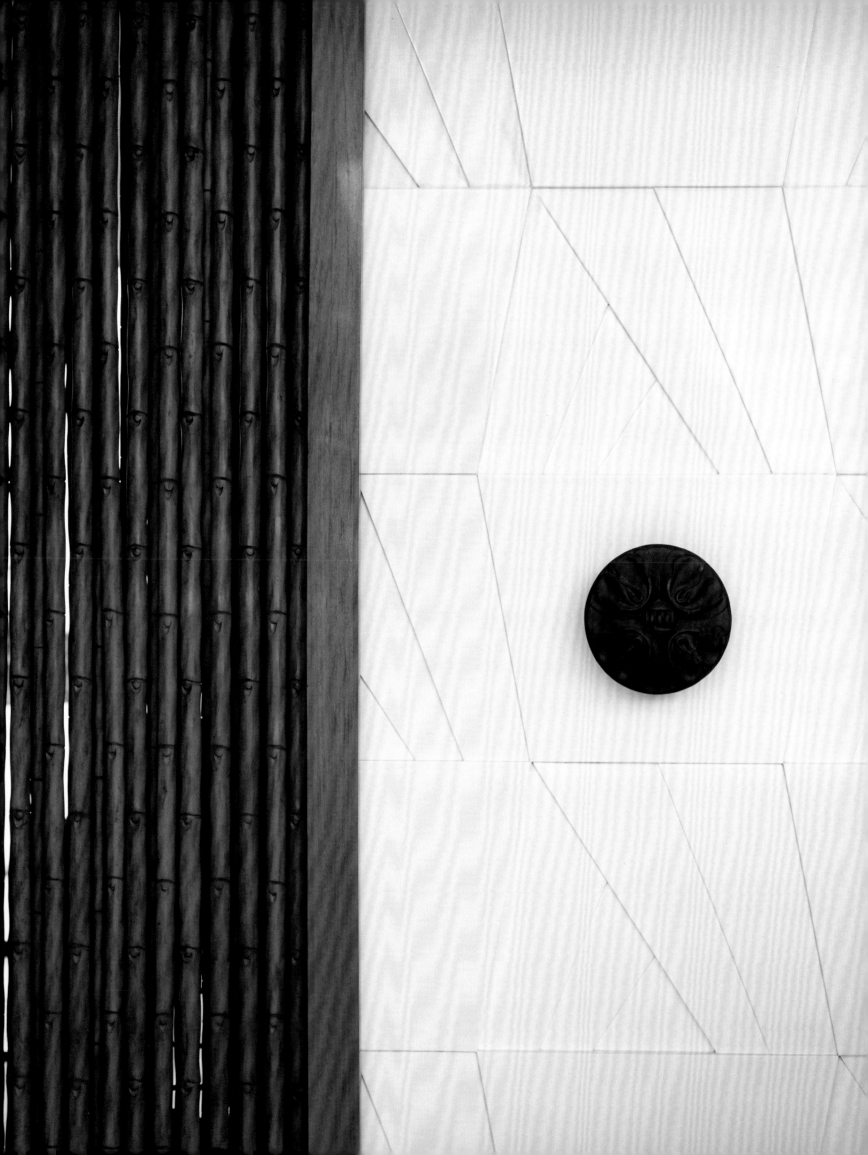

first place we experience the undulating forms of the buildings—designed by Dominican architect Antonio Segundo Imbert—whose contours mimic the liquid rhythm and ripple of the waves seen from this bluff high above the beach.

The sense of fluid circulation those contours elicit is essential to the family's style of entertaining. They welcome guests and gracefully lead them around curved passageways to discover what lies around each bend. Montoya highlighted the flowing, meandering lines of these contours by covering the dado of the walls with Portuguese blue-and-white tiles. "This immediately sets the color palette," he also notes.

Many of the furnishings are custom, such as the dining room's locally handcrafted fish chandelier and the double-sided sofa in the outdoor living room. "The two sides of the sofa accommodate more people," says Montoya, "and many of these furnishings are movable, to make them flexible for different-sized groups." Other pieces—the flame stitch–upholstered swivel chairs in the latter space, for instance—are from Montoya's designs for Century Furniture. And, of course, there is no shortage of global fabrics, case goods, and objects: rugs from Colombian weavers at Hechizoo, Moroccan pierced-brass chandeliers, and a colorfully ornate Indian chest in the entry to the master suite.

Texture is also of utmost importance in this environment, not only for its visual interest but also because it creates a tactility that feels inviting and comfortable for the homeowners' guests. Whether it is the combed plaster of the dining room walls, the woven rope used on a massive sitting room coffee table and a bedroom headboard, or the intricate beadwork on the sitting room ottomans—all of it contributes to a natural, down-to-earth atmosphere that is instantly relaxing. Who wouldn't want to be entertained here?

OPPOSITE: Montoya designed the front door's bronze hardware.
OVERLEAF: The living room palapa appears to float on an island surrounded by a pool tiled in shimmering cobalt-blue glass tiles.

OPPOSITE: The spindle-legged table near a sculpture by a local artist was found on the island. Flared column bases make it appear as if they "grow" from the floor. ABOVE: Portuguese tile wainscoting around a wall enclosing the kitchen establishes the blue-and-white palette. The Indian mirror and Asian console-cum-bar were sourced locally.

Montoya made the living room palapa a versatile space by designing movable two-sided sofas that could accommodate more people and pairing them with swivel chairs he designed for Century Furniture upholstered in a flame-stitch fabric. Under the thatched roof are locally woven baskets he transformed into pendant lighting.

OPPOSITE: An intentionally "random" grouping of rocks forms a "poetic transitional moment" from terrace to pool and from this level to steps leading to a lower floor.
OVERLEAF: The dining room is accessed from the living room palapa and pool area through custom doors of painted metal banana leaves with bespoke pulls.

ABOVE: The dining room is enveloped in combed-plaster walls anchored by grooved coralina stone baseboards. OPPOSITE: A Montoya-designed dining table made of *cacho* (horn) can be pulled apart into four smaller segments for more intimate dining. Overhead, he commissioned a metal chandelier with a gold-leafed interior.

Montoya gave each powder room its own unique character. CLOCKWISE FROM TOP LEFT: One features
a Moroccan mosque lantern, inlaid mirror, and a carved-rock sink. Another pairs a Mexican mirror
with a dresser repurposed as a vanity. Faux-wood-plank tile distinguishes another. And in a powder room
off a downstairs terrace, Moroccan tile and a perforated-wood screen impart North African flair.

PRECEDING PAGES: A white-painted bamboo bar with bistro stools serves the lounge area downstairs, created by a built-in sofa; local rattan chairs; occasional tables from Ilumel in Santo Domingo; and pendants by Hechizoo, a Bogotá-based weaving atelier represented by Cristina Grajales Gallery, New York. OPPOSITE: For the adjacent dining area, Montoya redesigned classic Mexican barrel chairs to have slanted backs, more comfortable proportions, and softer upholstery. ABOVE: Upstairs, Montoya deployed the same chairs in another al fresco dining area on the terrace of the dining palapa. The tables seat up to sixteen.

A spectacular polychrome Indian chest inlaid with mirrors greets us at the entry to the master
suite. To the left is the sitting room; to the right the bedroom. Atop the chest, chased Mexican silver
decorative objects bracket a Mexican clay sculpture whose colors rival the piece on which it sits.

ABOVE: At the entry to the master bedroom is a console table bearing more decorative Mexican ceramics. Behind it, the headboard of the bed reinterprets Mayan symbology into plaster forms that Montoya set in a wooden grid to create a screen effect. OPPOSITE: Montoya covered the master bedroom palapa walls with woven rattan. Over the bed, which is dressed in Central American textiles, is a plaster chandelier by Brooklyn-based artist Stephen Antonson.

OPPOSITE: The master bathroom is a white-on-white fantasy of plantation shutters, coral-framed mirrors, porcelain sinks, and a marble-topped vanity. ABOVE: Montoya slipcovered the wife's vanity in easily laundered canvas. OVERLEAF: Hechizoo made the custom rug in the master-bedroom sitting room, atop which Montoya accommodated a sectional sofa and intricately beaded ottomans around a mammoth dyed-and-woven-rope table. The canvases are by contemporary local painters.

ABOVE AND OPPOSITE: Montoya gave each guest room its own unique character, varying the color palette (here, pink-toned walls and curtains, as well as Colombian bed pillows and a coverlet in vivid orange and fuchsia). Monogrammed linens add an element of bespoke luxury. OVERLEAF: Lush foliage (*left*) is everywhere at the Casa de Campo residence. A guest room (*right*) boasts a pale yellow palette on walls and in the cotton dhurrie rug. An Indian mirror hangs over the Philippine mahogany four-poster bed.

PRECEDING PAGES: Bathrooms exhibit equally multifarious characters. The shower in this guest bathroom is tiled with a colorful star quilt motif. OPPOSITE: All bathrooms except one have lushly landscaped outdoor showers. This one, used by the boys in the family, is enclosed in coralina walls for privacy. ABOVE: Outside the boys' room is a sitting area assembled from locally commissioned wicker furniture. OVERLEAF: In the back of the house, a double-terraced lawn accommodates a soccer playing ground as well as this seating area created with a bench of naturally felled wood, flanked by white bougainvillea bushes in pots.

SURFSIDE
FLORIDA

Serving two masters is usually a chaotic and frustrating exercise. Fulfilling the requirements of both, especially when they are disparate or outright contradictory, requires a high level of diplomatic and aesthetic mastery. Juan Montoya's innate skills in these two areas result in seemingly effortless success. The two masters here were an important art collection and the owners' passion for boating and fishing.

The art collection included large-scale contemporary photography by Frieke Janssens, Luca Missoni, and David Yarrow; painting, sculpture, and mixed media works by Julian Voss-Andreae, James C. Christensen, and Rowan Mersh; and ancient artifacts from Egypt and China, as well as early twentieth-century works from Africa. Also in the mix: one of the largest collections of Barbie dolls in America. Except for Ran Ortner's painting of ocean waves—and perhaps a Barbie attired in *marinière* stripes if we look really hard—not one of these had anything to do with a seaside lifestyle. Water, of course, plays an enormous role in the site, an eighth-floor apartment in Richard Meier's glass-enveloped private residences at The Surf Club.

Montoya realized that this elevated perch, graced with wraparound terraces, was approximately the perspective of a guest aboard a luxury liner moored off the coast of Surfside, just north of Miami Beach. "I brought them the idea of creating an environment that conveyed the feeling of being on a yacht," says the designer. First, the floor plan he created by combining two apartments (totaling about thirteen thousand square feet) is open and free-flowing. Second, many spaces—the entry hall, his office, the family room, a bar—sport paneling of *afromosia* wood (also called African teak) polished to a glossy sheen reminiscent of seafaring vessel interiors. Lastly, in ways both subtle and more apparent, forms also evoke the home's aquatic proximity:

Architect Richard Meier was commissioned to design three new buildings as part of the revamping of The Surf Club in Surfside (north of Miami Beach), established in 1930 as a private membership club by the legendary rubber and tire magnate Harvey Firestone. The new complex includes a Four Seasons Hotel and two private residential towers, one of which boasts this sprawling apartment.

In the corridor leading from the elevator lobby, Montoya establishes a connection to the marine setting with custom-designed doors boasting a fish-scale motif and a wavy tile pattern on the floor that he repeated above in a lighting cove. Lobmeyr chandeliers illuminate art that includes Australian photographer Peter Lik's limited-edition sylvan scene *Inner Peace* and artifacts from Egypt's early dynastic period (3150–2686 BC).

Custom silver entry doors feature a fish-scale motif. Inside the entry hall, the tile floor, as well as an architectural element above it lining the corridor, mimics waves. There is an aquarium in the bar. Furniture silhouettes are rarely orthogonal, tending instead toward a more liquid curvaceousness. These strategies connect the interiors to their topographical surroundings.

The color scheme of blues, whites, and grays would seem to be implicit in this calculation, but it actually derives from the wife's favored palette. "The wife doesn't like anything too colorful," observes Montoya. "She dresses stylishly but simply, and she also didn't want any gold. She likes silver because it's not flashy." Chrome, polished or brushed, is far more prevalent. It is deployed on the base of living room coffee tables, the deco pendants in a gallery behind the kitchen (where Egyptian and Chinese artifacts, as well as hundreds of Barbies, are on display), in her spectacular master bathroom, as well as on the facing of support columns in the family room, and in both his and her offices. Polished chrome, as well as mirror on a dining sideboard and the double doors leading into the master suite, reflect the marine environs, further amplifying the connection.

Lighting plays a vital role not only in illuminating the artworks but also in complementing them as works of art in their own right. There are Austrian Lobmeyr chandeliers in the entry hall (replicas of the 1960s masterpieces created for New York's Metropolitan Opera House), a custom Studio Drift chandelier in the family room, a bespoke bronze-and-glass fixture by Los Angeles–based David Wiseman over the dining table, Parisian artisan Jeremy Maxwell Wintrebert pendants over the quartz bar, and Irish artist Niamh Barry sconces flanking the master bed. Each contributes to the jewel-box quality of the apartment.

From the corridor, one enters a bar that features an illuminated quartz surface trimmed in polished stainless steel. Behind it, an aquarium further highlights the apartment's relation to its setting, while overhead are handblown glass pendants by Jeremy Maxwell Wintrebert, commissioned through Galerie Carole Decombe in Paris. The barstools are Fendi Casa. Highly polished *afromosia* wood paneling, carried over from the corridor, evokes yacht interiors.

In the living room, Montoya contrasted the building's right angles with curvaceous forms. He designed the round rug and the sofas, which form graceful parentheses around a trio of custom coffee tables (atop one is a *pâte de verre* vase from Daum). On the channeled plaster wall that opens onto the dining room are a dozen variations of moon photographs by Luca Missoni.

ABOVE: A detail of the chandelier commissioned from Los Angeles–based artist and designer David Wiseman. RIGHT: *Ocean Waves*, a hyperrealist painting by Alaska-based Ran Ortner, hangs above a Lorin Marsh mirrored sideboard. Near the window is *Temporal Sitter*, a high-polish bronze sculpture by Irish artist Kevin Francis Gray. OVERLEAF: The dining room ceiling had to be structurally reinforced to bear the weight of Wiseman's chandelier, which hangs over an immense table designed by Montoya with silver inlay and sabots. Around it, he had John Boone chairs upholstered in horsehair.

Dominating one wall of the husband's office is a large-scale photo of Dinka herders in South Sudan by British photographer David Yarrow, in front of which is *Onah*, a bronze female nude by Julian Voss-Andreae and a pre–First World War artifact from Africa. Atop the Tai Ping custom carpet is a suede sectional sofa and, by the DDC desk, a trio of paintings by American artist James C. Christensen (1942–2017). Dutch sculptor Hanneke Beaumont created the work on the balcony.

Montoya designed custom pocket sliding doors for this office, which breaks up the expanses of polished *afromosia* wood with a pattern rendered in veneers atop polished sheets of stainless steel. Beyond these is the main living space and the Luca Missoni works, below which we can appreciate the designer's attention to detail in the polished metal baseboards.

RIGHT: A modular Molteni&C "Turner" sofa grounds the family room atop another custom Tai Ping carpet designed to resemble river rocks. Additional seating around the custom coffee table comes in the form of a pair of "Nautilus" chairs by Vladimir Kagan. The millwork holds a selection of the owners' enormous collection of African artifacts. White lacquer on the ceiling and polished metal on the columns amplify light.

OVERLEAF: A round Macassar ebony Lorin Marsh table surrounded by Minotti's "Aston" chairs sits under a Studio Drift chandelier from Carpenters Workshop Gallery (left). A Stephen Wilkes photo of Jerusalem (right) hangs nearby.

PRECEDING PAGES: The wall behind the Molteni&C/Dada kitchen, where Roche Bobois barstools pull up to the marble island, houses a gallery space leading to the master suite.
ABOVE: A rock crystal mirror and dramatic zebra marble wainscoting in a powder room.
OPPOSITE (CLOCKWISE FROM TOP LEFT): The mirrored, riveted dining room sideboard. John Boone chair at the dining area's smaller table. The Studio Drift chandelier made of bronze and light-emitting "dandelions." Inlaid silver bands on Montoya's black lacquer dining table.

OPPOSITE: The couple's cat sits at the bone and Macassar ebony desk in the wife's office opposite Lorin Marsh chairs upholstered in gray velvet mohair. The dog wearing sunglasses is actually an AeroBull audio speaker. ABOVE: In the gallery, Montoya designed shelves with glass, which can become opaque at the touch of a button, to display one of the largest collections of Barbie dolls in the world.

ABOVE: In a gallery before the master suite is a circa 250 BC Xian burial horse and more artifacts from Egypt's early dynastic period. Overhead, Montoya hung deco pendants from shallow coves in the ceiling.
OPPOSITE: Montoya designed the deco-style double doors that open into the master bedroom, which showcases custom work by the designer—a channel bed against a plush upholstered wall, nightstands (including hardware), and carpet—as well as a vintage chandelier from Todd Merrill Studio, New York.

On either side of the bed are dramatic ring sconces by Irish designer Niamh Barry. Fur pillows and throws adorn the bed and the double chaise longue, which was also designed by Montoya. Behind it is a Charles Paris "Ginkgo" lamp acquired through Donghia.

84

In the master bathroom, a wall of patterned blue glass panes set in polished nickel frames conceals her vanity area, a shower, and toilet. The custom mirror also features polished nickel framing. On the floor, Montoya designed a simple black trim that stands in for a runner. Another subtle detail: Montoya called for baseboards that curve upward to meet the walls. Overhead are vintage Venini chandeliers.

CAP CANA
DOMINICAN REPUBLIC

The power of seduction lies fundamentally in its ability to summon a sense of mystery. We are lured in gradually, calmly, helplessly—first with a taste of this, then a scent of that—until the spell is cast. It's a strategy as captivating in design as it is in romance, and one Juan Montoya deploys with skillful assurance. "It's always about what you will see when it opens up," he says of the increasingly revealing course he charted, architecturally and decoratively, through this property in Cap Cana, located on the eastern tip of the Dominican Republic.

As a result of the combination of interconnected structures by Dominican architect Antonio Segundo Imbert and lush jungle-like landscaping Montoya himself designed, the experience of this residence unfolds coyly as a succession of thatched palapas that are never fully revealed all at once. Rather, we discover them half hidden in a grove of palms, encounter them around a bend, or at the end of a walkway. By breaking the spaces up into separate buildings, Imbert disguised the considerable volume of the residence. "You feel each space more intimately that way," says Montoya (intimacy being, of course, another essential component of seduction). What unites the whole scheme is the material palette of coralina, palm thatch, and timber framing.

Montoya invokes a sense of arrival with a painted eighteenth-century double front door from Colombia's coffee-growing region, Valle Manizales, that is rich in texture and layers of distressed color. Set into a coralina wall and flanked by potted tree ferns, it opens onto a small courtyard that offers no hint of the panoramic ocean views beyond.

OPPOSITE: Looking out toward the Caribbean Sea is a large marble sculpture by Venezuelan sculptor Francisco Narváez (1905–1982). Montoya, who designed the verdant grounds, set it in a grass clearing surrounded by tropical foliage. Rain chains hang from the canopies of the various palapas that make up the house. OVERLEAF: "I suggested we do something sculptural and important at the entry," Montoya told his clients. That turned out to be a colorful distressed eighteenth-century door and frame (*left*) from Manizales, the main coffee-producing region in his native Colombia. On the door handles, he hung a necklace of pods and shells (*right*).

Easy linen-slipcovered
furniture beckons in an
interior living room anchored
by a massive wood table on a
sisal carpet. Behind the sofa
is a work by Ruud van Empel.
In the window bay, which is
dressed with two layers of
linen to create different
light-filtering options, are a
red Chinese console and
a metal strap pendant over a
bone-and-ebony table
and Anglo-Indian chairs.
A glass-fronted Philippine
cabinet is at left.

From here, visitors move along corridors and pathways that lead variously to graciously proportioned interior and exterior rooms. The indoor living room is vast, furnished with a comfortable linen sofa and armchairs around a massive plank coffee table. The airiness of the fabric and the woven texture of the sisal carpet impart a relaxed ambiance, while finer furnishings—a custom-designed ebony table with bone inlay surrounded by Anglo-Indian chairs, a glass-fronted display cabinet from the Philippines, and a red Chinese console—elevate the space.

Bedrooms are filled with exotic touches: a Chinese baldachin bed in a guest room also decorated with framed African textiles; an exquisite Indian tapestry repurposed into the stunning master bedroom headboard; a huge spherical pendant made of Balinese shells; and Mexican handwoven bed linens. Residents and guests dine outside in a separate palapa sited within a verdant stand of palms and elephant ear plants. It showcases a wall of coralina cut into tesserae to ramp up its tactility and a monumental custom copper chandelier that resembles an outsize cluster of sea grapes. The mixture of coarse and smooth surfaces, global artifacts and tropical greenery, is hypnotic.

The big reveal, however, is the enormous outdoor living room surrounded overhead by an open-air mezzanine. Here, alongside a cobalt-blue mosaic-tiled infinity pool, with the rhythmic insistence of the ocean beyond, the seduction is complete. By now we have traveled a winding, Edenic garden path. All that's left to do is make yourself comfortable.

OPPOSITE: For the master bathroom, Montoya employed local artisans to create a bamboo console topped with coralina stone and a hand-hollowed stone vessel sink. OVERLEAF: To ramp up the textural interest, Montoya created a wall of irregular travertine tesserae on which he hung slices of tree stumps and a cantilevered server (*left*). The McGuire chairs and stone table sit under a custom copper chandelier depicting seagrape plants. The property has stone paths that meander through a verdant tropical landscape (*right*).

RIGHT: In lieu of an impractical rug, Montoya defined the outdoor living room with a border of river stone mosaic. All the furniture, which he refers to as "very *Out of Africa*," is designed by Montoya and scattered with throw pillows from Andrianna Shamaris, New York. Overhead are Balinese baskets repurposed as light fixtures. OVERLEAF: A mustard-yellow guest bedroom telegraphs an exotic Asian feel with a Chinese baldachin bed, custom ebonized doors with bamboo patterning (*left*), and an elaborate Chinese console topped by a framed African textile (*right*).

98

PRECEDING PAGES: The beach at sunset (*left*) and a stair to the second level (*right*). Montoya suggested the lashing on the railings to add to the handmade treehouse look of the palapa.

RIGHT: Overlooking the outdoor living room is a mezzanine recreation area. Furniture is a mix of local and imported seating. The woven Colombian rug suggests an indigenous pattern, says Montoya, and brings color to the simple space.

OPPOSITE: Another second-floor lounging area, this one strung with a hammock. OVERLEAF: The white sand beach (*left*). In the master bedroom (*right*), Montoya used an Indian tapestry as a headboard for a bed dressed in embroidered Mexican textiles, which he set into a blue niche that highlights the tapestry. The massive pendant light was made from a Balinese shell sculpture. A parchment boudoir cabinet stands between the ebonized wood doors. PAGES 110–11: The *hamacario* (*left*) is an area strung with colorful Colombian hammocks, perfect for an afternoon nap. The blue volume (*right*) encloses a guest room.

PRECEDING PAGES: A corner of the outdoor living room looking out over the pool and the beach beyond. RIGHT: Blue mosaic tiles create a dramatic effect on the floor of the curved swimming pool, which follows the line of the beach.

MIAMI BEACH FLORIDA

Stylistic genres never disappear completely, evolving instead through time according to the fashions of the era. Art deco's 1920s French origins morphed endlessly, first into art moderne (or streamline moderne) in France in the 1930s, then into various regionalized permutations throughout the world. In the United States, Miami Beach was the epicenter of what many refer to as "tropical" art deco, so it is hardly surprising to find, rising at the rim of the city's Biscayne Bay, what might appear to be this residential homage to the style. Yet it is the genre's trajectory through Asia, in such places as Shanghai, Bombay, Singapore, Manila, and Bandung—an Indonesian city once known as "the Paris of Java"—that offer a more relevant context for art deco as the perfect foil for the treasure trove of Eastern art and artifacts behind the house's grandly pilastered facade.

The inspiration for the home was actually Angkor Wat, the Hindu temple complex begun in the early twelfth century by Suryavarman II, ruler of the Khmer Empire, which eventually evolved into a Buddhist holy site. Some later pilgrims believed Angkor Wat was built by a divine architect during the course of a single night. The homeowners, while not subscribing to this myth, nevertheless understood the mystical power of this architectural wonder to inspire such a legend. They hired architects at Miami-based Brockhouse Associates to create an imposing temple-like structure, refracted through an art deco prism, that would telegraph a similarly numinous sensibility to envelop their passionately amassed Asian collections—from Burmese *hsun-ok* offering vessels and Indian jali screens, to Thai Buddhas and antique Chinese wedding cabinets.

"I've designed a lot of homes in Paris buildings that date from the height of the art deco era," says Montoya. "But here, the mélange was more important

The inspiration for the house, realized with the help of architects Bruce Brockhouse and Al Naranjo of Brockhouse Associates in Miami, was the Hindu temple complex at Angkor Wat in Cambodia, where the homeowners had traveled. The entry features an impressive double-height custom door that conveys the enormous scale of the original Hindu structures.

The design team interpreted the Angkor Wat inspiration through the lens of art deco, which, Montoya notes, traced an influential path throughout the world, taking on various localized flavors (think Rabat, Bombay, Shanghai, and others). Here, it is reflected in flat roofs, rectilinear volumes, the use of black and white, the "X" motif on the doors and entry gate, streamlined pilasters, and the custom-designed lanterns flanking the gate.

118

than simply using pieces by Ruhlmann, Rateau, or Frank." Blue-chip specimens are here, of course, such as Lalique sconces above a pair of Raymond Subes consoles in the entry hall, both standing near a Lucien Gibert bronze of a woman. But more often than not, Asian elements and deco intertwine. Just beyond the entry hall, for example, we arrive through a Moorish arch at a corridor of checkered black and white marble lit by deco-style torch sconces of Montoya's design. The sconces flank an ancient stone altar table from a temple in southern India. To enter the dining room, we pass through a carved marble colonnade from India. Montoya framed the dining table, which he illuminated with a deco pendant and surrounded in 1960s chrome chairs, with two antique black linen chests from Hong Kong.

The pairing of Eurocentric and Asian architecture and decor becomes so seamless that Montoya could feel free to indulge in fantasias of each genre in certain rooms without upsetting the overall harmony of these juxtapositions. Some spaces might skew more thoroughly deco (the master bathroom and the wife's mirrored dressing room, which apparently led a former life as Jean Harlow's boudoir), while others embody a more resolutely exotic mood (a sitting room that appears to be inspired by one of the extravagant seraglios at Topkapi Palace in Istanbul).

Angkor Wat was meant to honor the omnipotence of Hindu, Jain, and Buddhist gods through architecture that symbolized their five-peaked home on Mount Meru. This distinguished residence in Florida honors something that is also eternal: the infinitely creative impulse of art and design—both Eastern and Western—to ennoble ordinary human life to something of ineffable beauty.

Black and white continues on the Turkish marble floors in the entry corridor, which provides the first glimpse of how Montoya mixed the sophistication and streamlined aesthetic of art deco with ancient treasures from throughout Asia. Here, the designer's custom torch sconces adhere to the former style, while illuminating a stone altar table from a southern Indian temple.

European deco style and Asian exoticism coexist in the grandly proportioned entry hall, where Lucien Gibert's bronze statue of a seated bather presides over the space. To her side, flanking the door to the bar, two Lalique sconces hang above a pair of antique Raymond Subes consoles. Reaching the bar requires passing through salvaged stone columns topped with intricate Corinthian capitals, beyond which we see an Indian window screen and a pierced-brass mosque lantern.

The Gibert sculpture, discovered at the Makassar-France gallery in Paris, ushers visitors from the entry hall into the living room, where an extra-long and deep custom sofa in Holly Hunt Ultrasuede (and accessorized with pillows in Lelièvre fabric) sits between deco-style end tables and lamps. Mirrors above the settees reflect the entry to the dining room at left and the library at right, both accessed through carved stone colonnades from India.

In the dining room, Montoya paired 1960s chairs found at the Miami Antique & Design Expo with a custom tufted banquette upholstered in Holly Hunt Ultrasuede. Above it is a digitally manipulated and enlarged print of a photograph the homeowner took in Africa and, on both sides, massive laundry chests from Hong Kong.

127

The library is painted a moody gray to create a warm, clubby atmosphere. The dark backdrop also serves to highlight such treasures as eighteenth-century Chinese demilune tables displaying Tang Dynasty animal sculptures, portraits of an Indian maharaja and maharani from the 1700s, and a Song Dynasty head on a pedestal by the window. The stools in front of the fire are 1930s art deco from Argentina.

The black-and-white scheme continues in the butler's pantry, which juxtaposes white walls with a dramatically veined black marble floor. Montoya hung a Frank Stella work over the sink. Overhead is a pair of 1920s German Bauhaus chandeliers—gleaming in chrome and black opaline glass—found in Argentina.

Hausscape, the custom
kitchen outfitters based
in Miami, executed
Montoya's design for the
cool-as-a-cucumber
kitchen, which is sheathed
completely in stainless steel.
For dining, he placed the
vintage chrome-and-glass
table and chairs alongside
a built-in banquette,
with seating upholstered
in Edelman leather.

OPPOSITE: Montoya transformed a second-floor corridor into a gallery. Along one side, a series of portraits by Suhas Bhujbal, a San Francisco Bay Area painter born in India's Maharashtra state; on the other, Venini sconces. A kneeling nun sculpture from Thailand meditates before an eighteenth-century Buddha from Ashwood Gallery, Bangkok. OVERLEAF: The master suite foyer features an eighteenth-century Tibetan Buddha head atop a 1930s ebony-and-opaline-glass table from the homeowner's collection. The elaborate art nouveau door leads to the bedroom. Chrome urns stand atop Macassar ebony pedestals next to a painting on wood by Balinese artist Nyoman Gunarsa (1944–2017), acquired from a gallery in Bali's artistic Ubud neighborhood, and two Aboriginal spears from Australia.

At the foot of the bed is
a seating area composed
of custom-designed chaises
in Holland & Sherry suede
and an antique Indian
maharaja bed-turned-table.
By the window, a nineteenth-
century Buddha reclines
on a Chinese console.

The wife's vanity area clearly led a previous life as Jean Harlow's dressing room. Reflective surfaces—mirror, polished nickel, highly lacquered wood—exude a sense of glamour. The mirror's deco-style sidelights look straight off the *Normandie*.

A white marble floor inlaid with a grid of black marble tiles in the master bathroom creates a graphic backdrop to a white tub and contrasting black lacquer cabinetry. Lucite pulls, towel bars, and sconces ramp up the deco chic. The carved glass sconces are Venini, while the 1930s chandelier above is by Venetian glassmakers Barovier & Toso.

A sumptuous retreat, located in the house's meditation tower, is layered with silks and appointed with an elaborate nineteenth-century Turkish enameled silver incense burner (on the marble table) and a nineteenth-century Moroccan carved wooden window. To illuminate the space, Montoya installed a rose-glass lantern purchased in Istanbul and an antique pierced-brass lantern from Doha, Qatar.

Indian carved-stone chairs
stand on either side of a water
wall cascading over black
marble tile. Nearby, offerings
of flowers are placed at the
foot of a stone sculpture
from Bali, which seems to
meditate placidly within
a niche formed by hedges.

146

The pool and outdoor
lounging area face Miami's
Biscayne Bay. Montoya
designed all the furnishings
and had them covered
in white to create an ethereal
mood that feels almost
like they belong on the deck
of an ocean liner. The
Moroccan lanterns, at right,
are antiques.

FISHER ISLAND FLORIDA

If, as they say, elegance is the privilege of age, this pied-à-terre in the exclusive enclave of Fisher Island would seem to attest to the persistence of this truth. "The clients are a Main Line Philadelphia couple in their sixties who use this as their winter retreat," says Montoya. "Because they entertain a lot and their children are gone, it is a very grown-up apartment with fine fabrics, many custom pieces, period antiques, and contemporary art."

Art deco, of course, is particularly well suited to the locale—the island sits off Miami Beach between Biscayne Bay and the Atlantic Ocean—though the examples on display here draw more heavily from the French iteration of the aesthetic than from Miami Beach's highly stylized tropical deco genre. "I tried to give more interior character to the apartment," says Montoya of the eight-thousand-square-foot residence. The first evidence of this, in the foyer, conjures a grand sense of arrival through the lavish use of stone. Each slab was personally chosen by the designer from quarries in Italy. Montoya defined the octagonal space with a multistepped ceiling overhead and, on the floor, a border of dark aggregate marble encircling a medallion pattern executed in other exquisite marbles. Baseboards are also stone, as are honey onyx panels lining niches for displaying pedestals and urns designed by Montoya. In the center is a glass pendant hanging over a center hall table, both of them period art deco.

A portal flanked by eucalyptus columns leads us into the main living area, a space originally segmented into separate rooms. Montoya removed doors that obscured views of adjacent rooms, expanding the space laterally into a kind of crescent-shaped enfilade. This provided a more panoramic view of the water. Lining up uninterrupted now along the windows are a media room, living room, bay-window alcove, dining room, and bar (spectacularly swathed in the same honey onyx previewed in the entry hall).

The apartment is on Fisher Island, which Carl Fisher bought in 1919 from Miami's first Black millionaire, Dana Dorsey, and turned into one of the richest zip codes in the United States. William Vanderbilt erected his mansion here in the 1930s. The elite roster of residents that followed has included Oprah Winfrey, Mel Brooks, Boris Becker, Caroline Wozniacki, and Julia Roberts.

Montoya ramped up the sense of depth and tactility by upholstering the primarily white furniture with a refined textural mix. He also indulged in sumptuous details such as the living room sofa's bullion fringe, a Fortuny chandelier and specimen marble table in the window alcove, tufting on the dining chairs, Lalique pendants and a Daum *pâte de verre* vase at the bar, and bone pulls on the eucalyptus millwork of the media room.

In the master suite, the overtly posh factor briefly goes subtly underground in exchange for a warm, monochromatic serenity. "I find that bedrooms with a lot of color bother me," says Montoya. So, here, sand-colored upholstered walls soften the envelope around a Louis XVI–style bed that rests against a channel-tufted panel of ivory silk. But glamour and grandeur are back in the master bathroom. Montoya combined three small rooms into one. Its circular configuration echoes the impressive foyer, as does the abundant use of stone—luminescent white onyx, which envelops the walls, vanity surfaces, and tub. The identical custom vanities feature dimensional drawer fronts with silver pulls and, overhead, another luxe deco chandelier hangs from a lacquered cove ceiling.

Clearly, Montoya has dispensed with all child's play. Every inch of this apartment telegraphs a consummate sense of mature sophistication. Its color palette of sandy hues, with pops of blue, connects the interiors to their natural surroundings, but the luxury of its appointments channels the fashionable métier of this seaside metropolis.

The octagonal foyer features beautifully figured stones purchased at quarries in Italy. The architectural scene depicted in the artwork was assembled with stone inlays in a technique called *pietra dura*, a decorative art that flourished in Florence during the Renaissance. An art deco chandelier hangs over a 1930s table from an ornately multistepped cove ceiling.

RIGHT: Visible from the doorway, through custom-designed eucalyptus wood columns, is the open-plan main living space. The foyer introduces honey onyx wall panels set into niches around the room. The use of this stone is carried into the larger living area's bar. OPPOSITE: Montoya designed the pedestals and the translucent glass urns, the latter sporting elongated neoclassical shapes popularized in the 1930s and '40s by French metalworker Raymond Subes.

RIGHT: Montoya illuminated the honey onyx panels of the bar to create a dramatic effect. The custom barrel-back barstools were inspired by art deco designs. Lalique light fixtures illuminate variously colored glassware. To the left is a *pâte de verre* vase by Daum. OVERLEAF: Montoya opened the living room up from formerly enclosed spaces to create a sense of flow. In the living area, a Belle Époque daybed sits in the foreground of a seating arrangement that emphasizes fine fabrics and luxurious details such as bullion fringe and button tufting. The blue painting and glass sculpture relate to the marine landscape outside.

RIGHT: The family room adjacent to the living room features a subtle paisley-patterned fabric on the custom sectional, a Patterson Flynn Martin rug, and eucalyptus paneling with bone pulls. Two James Mont chairs face the waterfront views across the room. OVERLEAF: Between the living room and dining room is a window bay where an upholstered banquette encircles a specimen marble table. Outside the dining room windows is a terrace with expansive Biscayne Bay views.

ABOVE: A classically chic Fortuny chandelier hangs in the window bay, where a deco games table is sometimes pulled in for checkers or backgammon. OPPOSITE: In the dining room, British Khaki dining chairs surround a deco table. The pendant overhead is also vintage deco. A custom silverleaf-framed mirror hangs over a circa 1940 sideboard. The dining table's centerpiece is a Dale Chihuly work in glass from his *Seaforms* series.

PRECEDING PAGES: Montoya encased the husband's library in recessed niches of satin burl wood millwork and confined the color scheme to sandy shades that echo the coastal beaches. The Macassar ebony desk is a bespoke design. Montoya found the 1950s armchairs at Galerie Patrick Fourtin, Paris. RIGHT: A Louis XVI–style bed infuses the master bedroom with a feminine feel, and balances more masculine elements such as the Biedermeier bedside chests and a 1970s bench. The shell lamps are also from Galerie Patrick Fourtin.

Montoya combined three rooms to create the extravagant master bathroom, which he swathed in gleaming white onyx. A deco fixture hangs from a recessed circular ceiling cove trimmed in cream-colored faceted plaster. The custom-designed lacquer vanity drawers with silver pulls have a pyramidal dimensionality. The transition from walls to floor is marked around the room by a wave-shaped baseboard in white onyx.

PUNTA MITA MEXICO
PUBLIC ROOMS

There are nights along this idyllic Mexican Pacific shore when the water comes alive with a phenomenon known as "sea sparkle." The source of this hypnotic bioluminescence is the *Noctiluca scintillans* (also called *Noctiluca miliaris*), a single-cell organism that floats in beds of phytoplankton and, when disturbed, emanates an otherworldly light. It is this magical marine denizen that gives this sprawling thirty-nine-thousand-square-foot compound—essentially a private resort for a couple and their four children—its name: Noctiluca.

Stylized depictions of this glowing sea fauna are carved into stone plaques set into the fourteen-foot ochre travertine walls that flank the entry to the residence. To reach the property, architect Mark de Reus heightened expectations by deploying "a progression of arrival experiences," he says. A drive through a grassy allée of approximately nine hundred palm trees leads to a motor court, then a climb up pyramidal steps conveys us through the travertine walls onto a *pasarela*, or gangway, hovering above shallow pools. The corridor's thatched roof is supported by naturally felled mahogany trunks wrapped with strangler fig vines known as *matapalo*. At the terminus is a "volcano" palapa, where guests can survey a one-thousand-foot-long coral beach.

"I wanted to create a village-like feel," says de Reus of this configuration of multiple palapas. Montoya emphasized this idea by giving each palapa—whether public or private—its own distinctive character, designing custom furnishings that he mixed with antiques and art indigenous to the region. "I spent one and a half years traveling from town to town in Mexico looking for artisans to produce the furniture so it would have an authenticity to its location," says Montoya. "So, everything has the flair and feeling of being in Mexico."

OPPOSITE: At the center and four corners of the motor court are banyan trees that will eventually canopy the entire space. Guests step from there into an entry corridor, or *pasarela*, where naturally felled mahogany trunks covered in strangler fig vines known as *matapalo* support a spectacular thatched roof. OVERLEAF: The pasarela is visible as the lateral structure in the upper right third quadrant on the aerial view and terminates at the so-called conical "volcano" reception palapa.

The pasarela's pathways, made of coralina stone with a black river rock trim, cross over interior pools. To the right is the entrance to the master suite and, beyond it, luxuriantly planted tropical gardens.

This sense of place was paramount for the design team, directed by the brief handed them by the client, who had a profound respect for the Mesoamerican cultures of Central America. Research into primarily Mayan architecture led to a hybrid of "modern and ancient sensibilities," explains de Reus—clean, rectilinear forms that also subtly referenced the stepped pyramids of the region's pre-Columbian ruins. These ochre travertine shapes were hand-chiseled to impart a sense of centuries-old wear, and also interspersed with concrete walls infused with earthy colors that "evoke the feel and depth of saturation used by Mayans that we discovered from our research." There are also notched detailing and carved symbols on various columns throughout that the team extrapolated from Mesoamerican motifs.

Like the architecture, Montoya's interior design represents a hybrid of ancient arts and modern living concepts. "You have to interpret cultures, not copy them," says the designer. "I hate to do something that forces a concept. We live in a time where function and comfort also have to be taken into account. A room has to smile at you, give you a sense of pleasure." A smile, of course, signals friendliness and welcome, a feeling Montoya conveys primarily through the comfortable tactility of handwoven fabrics, sisal rugs and natural materials like terra-cotta, wood, and warm metals such as hand-hammered copper. Seating in the main living palapa—drawn primarily from the estate sale of the famed Mexican midcentury modernist architect Francisco Artigas, except for a woven rattan sofa and a games table designed by Montoya—beckons with its roomy proportions, hand-carved wood, and folksy upholstery. Accompanying these are a seventeenth-century refectory table from Cuernavaca, pre-Columbian figures of painted terra-cotta, and other antiques.

For the dining room, Montoya found midcentury chairs that echo the tapered shapes of the surrounding pyramidal columns. Adorning them are copper inserts depicting various local flora and fauna. To light the scene, he repurposed Mexican fishing baskets into pendant fixtures and installed gas-fired torches around the room. More indigenous artistry covers a wall above a suspended console in the form of colorful ceramic plates featuring elaborately painted floral patterns.

The combination of architecture and interiors unequivocally lands us in this specific setting at this particular time, invoking the powerful history and mythology of the region in a way that is contemporary and suited to modern living.

The "volcano" palapa functions as a reception area where guests can view the pool area and the one-thousand-foot stretch of beach beyond. A painted Mexican vase on a circular table anchors the space. Montoya worked with artisans in Mexico to produce rattan furniture of his design.

ABOVE AND OPPOSITE: Blue serpentine walls meander through verdant gardens at various points throughout the property. According to architect Mark de Reus, they were a feature of Mayan architecture, representing the river of life and its flow to the sea. They also echo the pattern of the waves.

ABOVE: Francisco Zúñiga (1912–1998), the Costa Rican–born Mexican sculptor, once said that he preferred figurative art because it was "the most important aspect of the world around me." Here, one of his bronze works features a group of noble pre-Columbian figures. OPPOSITE: Another view of the sculpture, whose figures seem to be contemplating the ocean, through a stone portal.

A stairway leading to the rooftop lounging area of the family room, which de Reus refers to as the "storm room" due to its function as a place the family can retreat during inclement weather. The ochre travertine walls were hand-chiseled to create a more rustic texture on the stairway's interior walls, a contrast to a smooth monolithic railing carved directly into the wall. The notch detail on the corners is repeated throughout the complex.

ABOVE: Set into the ochre travertine walls is a carved stone plaque depicting a stylized version of *Noctiluca scintillans*, the luminescent single-celled sea organism that gives the residence its name. At the base of the walls is a sculpture of a jaguar, the ruler of the underworld in Mayan mythology and a symbol of power, ferocity, and luxury. OPPOSITE: Architect de Reus played with pyramidal shapes to evoke the Mesoamerican structures of the Mayans, Aztecs, and Zapotecs.

PRECEDING PAGES: Colorful JANUS et Cie umbrellas provide shade for teak lounge chairs designed by Montoya. ABOVE: More custom rattan furniture by the pool, which features more pyramidal volumes around its perimeter. OPPOSITE: An indigenous wattle overhead breaks up sunlight in the lounge area, which features an onyx bar that Montoya cleverly illuminated. Behind it, the "volcano" reception palapa.

ABOVE: Indigenous wattle over an outdoor dining area. OPPOSITE: Around the pool are several lounging and dining areas. Montoya designed the live edge table and benches that sit poolside, and decked the table in abundant bouquets of variously colored bougainvillea plants that grow all over the property.

The living room palapa steps down to a lounge area, which in turn steps further down to the infinity edge pool, which cascades over its ochre travertine borders into a catch basin for recycling. The red wall to the left of the palapa leads to the powder room.

PRECEDING PAGES AND ABOVE: The living room palapa gathers together Montoya's own custom rope-and-wood sofa (with the designer's own custom striped fabric) and various armchairs and another sofa purchased at a sale of the estate of famed Mexican midcentury modernist architect Francisco Artigas. A colorful Clarence House textile covers the sofa. Atop a refectory table from Cuernavaca, Montoya arrayed various antiques, including pre-Columbian figures and a massive painted Mexican vase. OPPOSITE: Artigas estate sale chairs surround a custom games table.

OPPOSITE: The owners requested an aquarium, so Montoya designed one into one corner of the living room, encasing it in a circular wood column. It is visible from the pool and serves to connect the structure to the ocean beyond. The seating arrangement sits on top of a casual sisal rug, which heightens the textural mix of the space.
OVERLEAF: The room's roof understructure of rafters and purlins, which support the palm thatch above.

ABOVE AND OPPOSITE: The architect researched Mayan colors to come up with the earthy red and yellow of the curved walls that lead to a powder room between the living and dining palapas. He saw this as the wellspring of the house, which he represented with a "pool" of river rock patterns at the base of the main ochre travertine wall, which also features a quoin decorated with Mayan symbols. OVERLEAF: In the dining room, copper plates in the midcentury chairs depict local flora and fauna. Gas torches on the support columns of the palapa offer a note of theatricality to lighting that also includes a fixture, over the table, made from Mexican fishing baskets.

PUNTA MITA MEXICO
PRIVATE SPACES

In a way, we owe our modern ideas of comfort to French architect Augustin-Charles d'Aviler, who in 1691, when describing different kinds of residential rooms, distinguished between what he called *appartements de parade* and *appartements de commodité*. Though this residence is—as any beachside getaway should be—thoroughly informal and relaxing, it too follows a certain design hierarchy. Public rooms are laid-back versions of the *appartements de parade*, "grander and more impressive in scale, more elevated and refined," says Montoya. The private spaces, on the other hand, hew more closely to the intention of d'Aviler's *appartements de commodité*. They are, says the designer, "lighter and cheerier, though I'd be happy to be in any one of them."

Poised somewhere between these two concepts is the master palapa, which retains the scale and the refinement of its art and furnishings, while still radiating a sense of serenity and restfulness. A coral stone corridor on a perpendicular axis to the entry pasarela leads to weighty wooden doors designed by Montoya. Their heft and decoration of hammered copper straps, rivets, and plates announce the room's importance in the pecking order of private quarters. Inside, a console bears a collection of copper vases, above which hangs a painting by Rufino Tamayo (1899–1991), the Zapotec-descended master who helped define the character of Latin American modernism in art, which synthesized traditional Mexican imagery with twentieth-century movements such as cubism and surrealism.

Another set of wood and copper doors leads into the master bedroom. The space announces a layout that Montoya repeats throughout the sleeping palapas. Upon entering, we find ourselves at the back of the bed. "That puts those living or visiting here closer to the water and the view when they wake up," he says. The headboard serves dual functions as a screen that pauses our arrival—helping segue

OPPOSITE: A vignette in the master bedroom suite illustrates Montoya's confident approach to pattern and color. Others might have used any one of these items singly—an antique Mexican framed textile, painted vase, and colorful cabinet—but he brings them together and allows the grouping to create its own idiosyncratic relationship. OVERLEAF: The private quarters are located on the lower left (master bedroom suite and girls' rooms) and upper right (guest rooms and boys' quarters) in this aerial view of the property.

us more gracefully into the relaxed intimacy of the bedroom—and also partially reveals water views through plaster casts of abstracted pre-Columbian motifs.

Inside is a circular space, the roof supported on monumental pyramidal stone columns into which pocket doors can slide, opening the room to the outside. There is more high-caliber art: a pair of Tamayos flanking the entry doors, and a sculpture by Ángel Botello (1913–1986), the Spanish–Puerto Rican artist dubbed "the Caribbean Gauguin." There are also Frank Lloyd Wright nightstands and an extravagantly carved and gilded daybed, produced in Mexico sometime during the overlap of Victorian and art nouveau periods, which cradles the body on the backs of majestic, larger-than-life falcons. Montoya checked the exuberance of the latter gesture with sisal rugs and bed linens handwoven in Mexico. All the sleeping palapas, ten bedrooms in all, feature these two elements as well, plus private patios and interior sitting rooms. In the girls' rooms, the textiles tend to be more whimsical, sporting octopi and fish.

There are many other private spaces that guests rarely see. Most significant is what architect Mark de Reus calls the "storm room" because it is built with concrete ("the go-to material used in Mexico because it is able to withstand substantial loads and tolerate heavy wind and seismic activity") and impact-resistant glass. We are in hurricane country, after all. The space is, essentially, a family room with a lounging area, a billiard table, and a games table that occasionally doubles as a spot for casual dining. Straddling these areas is an enormous, showstopping canvas of a blue whale.

There is also a spa and fitness palapa and an entire complex for support staff and storage. Throughout the property, undulating walls mimic the waves splashing onto the cove's private beach, further contextualizing the estate to its locale. It is, in every sense of the word, a tropical Eden, a place where the world evaporates from consciousness and the family can subsume themselves in the beauty of nature, grand contemporary architecture, and Montoya's exquisite interior scheme.

A teak window and lattice panel at once frames a view to the lush tropical garden outside the master bedroom suite and offers a backdrop for an antique Mexican painted terra-cotta vessel. One of the property's wavy blue walls is visible beyond the greenery.

RIGHT: To the left of the entry pasarela, another path leads to the master bedroom suite. Solid teak doors echo the notch-carved wall quoins found around the property. Under the portal to the right is the entry to the suite.
OVERLEAF: Passing through the portal, the path terminates in a garden where large urns lining it direct visitors to a walled circular courtyard anchored by totem-like sculptures.

ABOVE: In the master bedroom palapa, we encounter a copper sculptural plate by Zúñiga set into a niche in an olive-green wall. OPPOSITE: Against the wall is an ornately carved Indian table purchased in Mexico, which supports a quartet of bright, floral-painted Mexican urns. OVERLEAF: This passageway in turn opens into a more interior space where another console (*left*) offers a display area for a collection of hammered copper vases in front of a Rufino Tamayo painting. Montoya designed the ornate doors (*right*), which he adorned with copper plates, straps, and rivets.

OPPOSITE: The master palapa roof is held aloft by massive pyramid-shaped columns with the same notched adornment on the quoins. De Reus had large cavities carved into them to accommodate the retractable glass-paneled doors, thus opening the space to the outdoors. ABOVE: The headboard screen is composed of blocks inspired by similar ones the design team saw at the National Museum of Anthropology in Mexico City.

At the foot of the bed is an extravagantly ornate daybed made in Mexico around the turn of the nineteenth to twentieth centuries, during the overlapping Victorian and art nouveau periods. On both sides of the custom leather and suede bed, Montoya echoed the lavish ornament with Mexican mercury glass lamps but balanced it with simple, rectilinear nightstands by Frank Lloyd Wright. A pair of Tamayo works flanks the entry behind the headboard screen.

224

ABOVE: To one side of the bed is a bronze sculpture by Ángel Botello, the Spanish–Puerto Rican artist dubbed "the Caribbean Gauguin," on a Mexican carved table that keeps company with an equally sculptural modern Mexican rope chair. OPPOSITE: The bed and lounge chair are dressed in custom woven fabrics by Mexican artisans whom Montoya discovered while traveling the villages of the country for over a year before the project started.

OPPOSITE: De Reus designed chunky, rough-cut onyx wall lights that emit a subtle glow, then repeated them throughout the outdoor spaces of the entire property. ABOVE: In the master suite's sitting room, more custom woven fabric covers a bespoke sectional sofa. The deco table in the corner was purchased locally, but the lamp came from a gallery in Paris. The panel on the wall is by Monterey, Mexico–born artist Alfredo Ramos Martínez (1871–1946).

ABOVE AND OPPOSITE: The master bathroom mixes coralina with salmon walls of smooth, lightly buffed plaster, which undulate around a tub and vanity of deep Moroccan blue. Montoya adorned the space with indigenous pottery and baskets and a polished chrome porthole-style vanity mirror.

ABOVE: For the girls' rooms, Montoya channeled a more lighthearted mood, commissioning fabrics embroidered with sea creatures, such as these rosy red octopi. OPPOSITE: In one of the girls' rooms, fanciful yellow fish cavort on the beds. The room also contains whimsical painted Mexican chests, colorful artwork, and an antique pull-toy horse.

RIGHT: A trio of guest palapas cluster together between the boys' palapas and the spa and fitness area. Each has its own terrace, but they share common lounging and recreational spaces between them. OVERLEAF: Montoya wanted each guest room to have its own particular character, so he varied finishes and color schemes. This one's wealth of warm wood relies on multihued folk motifs embroidered against beige grounds for its punches of color.

RIGHT: Canary yellow is the dominant color in another guest room, its brightness enhanced by brilliantly painted Mexican trunks repurposed as bedside tables.
OVERLEAF: The girls share a living space that is part inside, part outside. It includes a table for games or eating (*left*) and, against one wall (*right*), a juxtaposition of a seventeenth-century Mexican candelabrum and Aztec warrior prints.

238

ABOVE: Fragrant frangipani blossoms float in a bowl, scenting the air. OPPOSITE: A nineteenth-century Mexican poncho hangs above a colorful built-in sofa in a common space. OVERLEAF: The boys' room (*left*), as in other family and guest palapas, has beds that sit on stone plinths. The dominant hue here is sapphire blue, which is accented with more colorful folk weavings. Banana leaf palms (*right*) catch the light, seeming almost as if they glow.

PRECEDING PAGES: The veranda of a guest palapa. ABOVE: A contemporary French light fixture hangs above the games table in the family "storm room." OPPOSITE: Beneath a Blatt billiard table is a Moroccan rug and on the wall, above an antique Mexican water jug, is an impressive depiction of a majestic blue whale.

ABOVE: The boys' bathroom picks up the avocado green seen on the other side of the property in the entry hall to the master suite (pages 218–19). Here it's used on hand-poured concrete sinks and a cantilevered shelf on the wall. OPPOSITE: Outside this bathroom, the color continues on the walls of a lushly planted outdoor shower.

In the evening, the uplit thatched palapa ceiling creates a magical sense of welcome at the entry to the residence from the motor court. On either side of the opening between hand-chiseled ochre travertine walls are stone plaques with carvings depicting stylized images of the *Noctiluca scintillans*, the bioluminescent sea creature that gives the property its name.

ACKNOWLEDGMENTS

Any designer owes the publication of a monograph first and foremost to his clients. I give my thanks to the owners of the properties featured here, without whose unqualified support, trust, and adventurous spirit this book would never have come to be. I would also like to acknowledge Urban Karlsson, my partner in work and life, who has been essential to the firm for decades and had an incalculable influence on the book you hold in your hands.

Also, I extend gratitude to Alison Newman in my office, who provided indispensable logistical assistance that ensured the smooth coordination of all components that compose this volume. Of course, no designer works alone. My entire staff deserves thanks for the extraordinary amount—and quality—of the work they have done over many years to help each and every project come into splendorous fruition.

I owe an immense debt of gratitude to my editor, Philip Reeser, who is responsible for conceiving this book from the beginning and working with great thoughtfulness and understanding to create results even better than I could have imagined. I am also thankful to publisher Charles Miers and the entire Rizzoli team, especially the book's talented designers, Doug Turshen and Steve Turner, who created something that is truly sumptuous to behold, and Jessica Napp, who facilitated my introduction to the publishing house.

It has been a pleasure to work with Jorge S. Arango, a skilled writer with a vast knowledge of art and design—and a true gentleman. I am impressed by how he captures the essence of a project and translates the work of contributing artists and artisans cohesively and with precision.

Photographers are the sum and substance of a monograph. Eric Piasecki and I have worked together often enough that I have come to appreciate and trust that he will see each project as if through my own vision, particularly when I cannot be present at a shoot. He is like my third eye. Jean-François Jaussaud has shown me how to perceive my projects in new ways, and the sophisticated perspective of Miguel Flores-Vianna has taught me so much about how three-dimensional space relates, and translates, to photography. Ken Hayden, a resident of South Beach, has a gift for capturing the light and tropical chic of Florida's coastal communities. While on the subject of Florida, I would be remiss in not thanking Bilal Barakat for his indispensable help with handling all the technical architectural aspects of the Surfside apartment. He has been an esteemed collaborator on other projects as well. And thanks, also, to Shaler Ladd III for his architectural expertise on the Bay Road project.

Last but not least, I am thankful for the many editors who have supported my career by presenting my work to a wider audience through their pages. Among them, I must single out Wendy Goodman, who so graciously agreed to write the foreword to this book. I am humbled to acknowledge the many talented people who have made this beautiful book a reality. I hope you will enjoy what you find here.

—*Juan Montoya*